RAINFORESTS

BY

MIKE CLARK

©2017
Book Life
King's Lynn
Norfolk PE30 4LS

ISBN: 978-1-78637-168-3

Written by:
Mike Clark

Edited by:
Charlie Ogden

Designed by:
Drue Rintoul

CONTENTS

Words in **bold** are explained in the glossary on page 31.

Habitats and Biomes

WHAT ARE HABITATS?

Habitats are places where plants and animals live. Habitats can include everything from mountains and rivers to deserts and oceans – even other living things!

The animals and plants that live in a habitat usually become **adapted** to it. This means that they become very good at raising their young and finding food and water in their specific habitat. A habitat can also keep the animal safe from **predators**, often by having lots of places to hide. This helps animals to **reproduce** safely.

Mountain goats have great balance and can jump large distances from rock to rock. Up here it is safe, as predators cannot travel along the rocks as fast as the goats can.

Mountain Goats

Animals that only live on other living things are called parasites. Aphids are parasites because they live on plants and take food away from the plants.

Aphids

WHAT IS A BIOME?

A biome is a very large area of the world where the **climate** is very similar. Because biomes are so huge, they usually contain many different habitats. As a biome's climate is the same all the way across it, many of the animals and plants that live in the same biome will adapt similar **traits**, even if they live in very different habitats. While some animals and plants are able to live in different habitats within the same biome, most living things can only live in one habitat.

For example, cactus plants can survive in dry deserts because they can store water. This helps them to survive long periods without rain. But in the rainforest, the cactus would not survive. Other plants would grow over the top of the cactus, blocking out the sunlight that the cactus needs to survive.

Some plants survive better in the dry, sunny conditions in the desert, whereas other plants survive better in the dark, damp conditions in the rainforest. This shows how living things adapt to their environment.

5

What Is a Rainforest?

A rainforest is a biome. Rainforests are areas that are covered by many trees and get lots of rain and sunshine. The average rainforest will receive up to six metres of rainfall a year! Rainforests also receive around 12 hours of sunlight a day.

All this water and sunshine makes the rainforest a perfect environment for trees. Because of this, rainforests are often filled with trees and other plants that are all fighting to get as much water and sunlight as possible. In rainforests, the plants fight to grow over each other as they try to get more sunlight.

The redwoods that grow in the temperate rainforests of North America can grow up to 90 metres tall.

Amazon Rainforest
Size: 5,500,000 km²
Yearly rainfall: 225 cm

Pacific Temperate Rainforests
Size: 295,000 km²
Yearly Rainfall: 200 cm

TYPES OF RAINFOREST

There are two main types of rainforest: tropical rainforests and temperate rainforests. Most of the rainforests around the world are tropical rainforests, which means that they sit on or near the **equator**. This area of the world gets lots of sunshine and rain.

Temperate rainforests are less common. They are found farther away from the equator in **temperate zones**. These rainforests grow in special areas between oceans and tall mountains. Being trapped between an ocean and mountains makes these areas warm and wet, just like the areas around the equator.

The Ghats Montane Rainforests
Size: 22,600 km²
Yearly rainfall: 250 cm

Taiheiyo Pacific Rainforest
Size: 138,300 km²
Yearly rainfall: 400 cm

Congo Rainforest
Size: 3,700,000 km²
Yearly rainfall: 200 cm

Indonesia and Malaysia Rainforests
Size: 165,100 km²
Yearly rainfall: 200 cm

Temperate
Tropical

Daintree Rainforest
Size: 1,200 km²
Yearly rainfall: 200 cm

Levels of the Rainforest

Emergent Layer

The rainforest is divided into four main levels. Each level of the rainforest gets a different amount of sunlight. The emergent layer is at the very top of the rainforest. This is the level of the rainforest that gets the greatest amount of sunlight. The trees that are able to grow all the way up to the emergent layer are rewarded with more sunlight.

Amazon Rainforest, Brazil

Canopy

The canopy is the part of the forest that is just below the emergent layer. The leaves above the canopy give the animals that live here shade from the sun. As the canopy is so high up, living up here protects animals from the many predators down below. It's the perfect habitat for insects, birds and **primates** that can eat the fruit, nectar and leaves that are easily found in the canopy layer.

This keel-billed toucan is perched on a palm tree in South America.

UNDERSTOREY

The understorey is the area of the rainforest between the ground and the canopy. Many **climbing plants** grow here as well as some ferns and small trees. It is also a great place for animals that want to escape danger on the ground.

These liana plants in Thailand are twisting their way up to the canopy.

FOREST FLOOR

The forest floor is below the understorey and it is the wettest part of the rainforest. Because of this, the forest floor is the perfect place for living things that like damp habitats. Fungi, which usually only grows in damp habitats, can be found all over the forest floor.

This toadstool is growing on the forest floor in a rainforest in Ecuador.

EMERGENT LAYER

Plants use sunlight and water to make food. This process is called **photosynthesis**. As there are a lot of plants in rainforests, they have to fight each other to get to the top before other plants grow over them and block out the sunlight. Those trees that grow above all the others are called emergents.

The tallest tree found in tropical rainforests is the kapok tree. These trees can grow up to 61 metres tall. The tallest tree in the world, the redwood, is found in the Pacific temperate rainforests and can grow up to 90 metres tall.

The kapok can grow as fast as four metres a year and can live to be 300 years old.

THE CANOPY

One thing that makes the trees in the canopy such a good habitat for animals is the amount of food that can be found here. The trees make fruit so that the animals will eat them and spread their seeds around the forest. There are thousands of different **species** of fruit tree in the rainforest and most of the animals in the canopy need this fruit to survive.

Starfruit

Ice Cream Beans

Chico Sapodilla

Limes

Papaya

Breadfruit

Wampee Fruit

Watermelon

Pili Nuts

Coconut

This market stall is filled with many different kinds of fruit that can be found in rainforests around the world.

Animals of the Canopy

The Flyers

The most common adaptation for animals in the canopy layer is the ability to fly. Many different insects, birds and bats fly around this layer of the rainforest to find food. Flying foxes, which can have a **wingspan** of up to 1.5 metres, are the largest bats in the world and are found in different rainforests across Africa, Asia and Australia.

Flying foxes can fly at speeds of up to 50 kilometres an hour.

Most of the animals in the canopy have adapted to be able to eat the fruit and nectar in the trees. However, there are many birds that also eat the insects in this layer of the forest. Eating the insects in their habitat has given some birds a secret **poisonous** defence against predators. The birds eat poisonous insects and store the poison within their bodies, which then seeps out of their skin and feathers.

This is a pitohui found in Papua New Guinea. Simply touching its feathers can cause a painful itch.

THE CLIMBERS

The canopy is also filled with many animals that cannot fly. These animals are often expert climbers. Gibbons are perhaps the best primate climbers in the world. They have adapted to have very long arms and legs, as well as a tail that can grip onto branches. Gibbons can swing through the forest at speeds of up to 56 kilometres an hour and can jump distances of up to 15 metres.

White-Handed Gibbon

Understorey

Not all of the plants in the rainforest can grow as tall as kapok trees. Instead, many have adapted special ways of climbing. Liana vines grow long, winding vines that wrap around nearby trees and slowly grow up them, towards the sunlight.

Because every plant is trying to get as much sunlight as possible for themselves, some climbing plants kill the tree that they are growing up. This is because there will be more sunlight for the climbing plant if the other tree dies. One such climbing plant is the strangler fig tree, which grows in parts of Asia and Australia. This plant slowly kills the tree that it is climbing up by strangling it and taking its place.

This cypress tree is being strangled by a strangler fig tree.

Monkey Ladder Liana Vines, Thailand

14

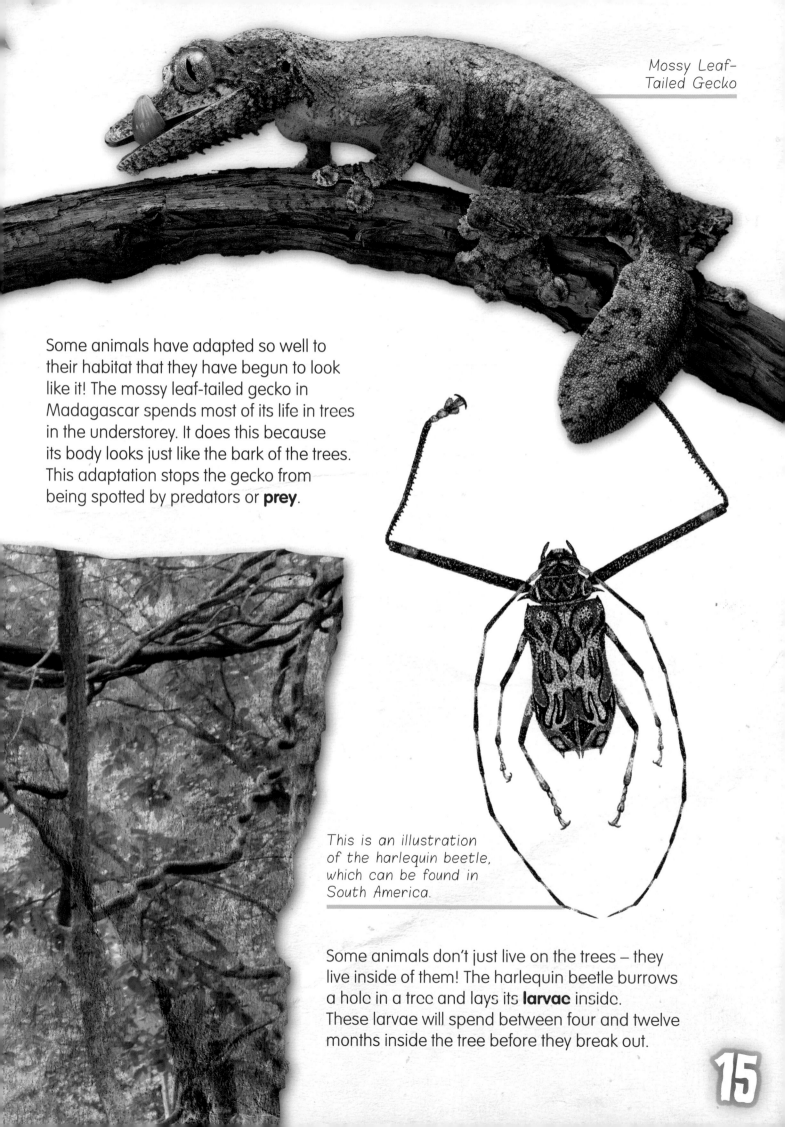

Some animals have adapted so well to their habitat that they have begun to look like it! The mossy leaf-tailed gecko in Madagascar spends most of its life in trees in the understorey. It does this because its body looks just like the bark of the trees. This adaptation stops the gecko from being spotted by predators or **prey**.

This is an illustration of the harlequin beetle, which can be found in South America.

Some animals don't just live on the trees – they live inside of them! The harlequin beetle burrows a hole in a tree and lays its **larvae** inside. These larvae will spend between four and twelve months inside the tree before they break out.

15

Forest Floor

The forest floor is home to thousands of insects that are very well adapted to their habitat. The most common type of insect in the rainforest is the ant. There are also many strange types of beetle on the forest floor, such as the rhinoceros beetle, which hides in fallen leaves and logs.

*Leaf cutter ants collect thousands of leaves during the day and feed these leaves to a friendly fungus. The fungus then provides the ants with an **antibiotic** that kills unfriendly fungi.*

Rhinoceros Beetle

Small plants on the rainforest floor also create the perfect habitat for very small animals. The strawberry poison dart frog, for example, raises its young in a small pool of water trapped in a flower or leaf. Here, the young are safe from being eaten by the fish that in live the rainforest's rivers.

Strawberry Poison Dart Frog

Big Cats

Leopards and jaguars also live on the forest floor, looking for prey. These big cats are very well adapted to their habitats. Both have spotted fur that helps them to hide in the shadows when hunting prey. They also have amazing eyesight and sharp claws, which makes it easier for them to find and catch food.

Although these cats are powerful predators, it does not mean that they are always safe. Other cats may attack them to get their food or to protect their area of the rainforest. To defend themselves from surprise attacks, the big cats sleep and eat in trees.

You can tell the difference between a jaguar and a leopard using their spots. Both cats have dark, rose-shaped spots, but a jaguar's spots have smaller dots inside of them.

From a distance, the pattern on the leopard's fur looks like the shadows of leaves hitting a branch.

Skilled Hunters

SNAKES

Big cats aren't the only big predators that hide in rainforest trees. Rainforests are also full of big and deadly snakes. The largest snake in the world is the green anaconda. It can be found in the Amazon rainforest and it can grow to be as much as seven metres long.

Although anacondas do hunt on land, they actually prefer the water and are excellent swimmers. The swamps and streams are the perfect habitat for the anaconda to hunt in as they attract many different animals to eat, such as birds and pigs that are looking for food and water to drink.

A green anaconda swimming underwater.

Green Anaconda

CHIMPS

A chimpanzee communicating with its relatives.

Chimpanzees have adapted to their habitat in a very special way. While some animals have adapted to be stronger, bigger or faster, the chimpanzee has instead adapted its behavior. Chimpanzees often live in big groups, called troops, and can communicate with each other using loud calls. These calls not only help them to warn each other of predators, such as an approaching jaguar, but also helps them to team up and hunt down small monkeys in the canopy.

Plants and Fungi

In crowded rainforests, colourful flowers sometimes aren't enough to catch the attention of **pollinating** insects. Because of this, some plants on the rainforest floor make a very strong smell to attract insects. One plant that does this is the titan arum. It grows up to three metres tall and smells like rotting meat.

The flowers in rainforests don't always use insects for pollination. Due to the lack of sunlight in rainforests, some plants have adapted flowers that can **digest** insects. Pitcher plants attract insects with small amounts of nectar and then catch them in their bell-shaped flowers. The flower has smooth edges, which makes it hard for the insect to climb out, and it is filled with an **acid** that helps to digest the insect.

The titan arum flower takes as long as ten years to grow.

The Nepenthes attenboroughii is the largest pitcher plant in the world.

Another insect eating plant, the Venus flytrap, will trap insects in its leaves. When the insect becomes trapped in its leaves, it is slowly digested by the plant.

Fungi generally grows in warm and damp habitats with lots of dead plants, which makes the rainforest floor their perfect habitat. But competition in the rainforest can be tough, so many fungi have adapted special ways of spreading their **spores**.

The most horrible method that a fungus uses to spread its spores is probably that used by the zombie fungus. Their spores can infect an ant and take control of its mind. Once the ant is under the control of the fungus, it will be forced to climb to the top of a tall plant. At this point, the ant will die and the fungus will grow a stalk out of the ant's head that releases a cloud of spores, infecting even more ants.

This zombie fungus has begun to grow out of the head of an ant.

Rivers, Swamps and Streams

Rainforests often contain rivers, swamps and streams. These habitats are filled with many large predators that can hide in the murky waters. The Amazon river dolphin is an expert hunter. It has adapted to have a much more flexible neck than most dolphins, which allows it to change direction very quickly in order to catch fish.

Amazon River Dolphin

Caiman

Swamps are shallow, meaning that large fish don't live in them. However, they make the perfect habitat for caimans. This predator hides in the plants and **algae** as it moves towards its prey. Caimans often sneak up on animals drinking from the swamp and grab them.

Red-Bellied Piranha

Streams are smaller than rivers meaning that they are usually home to smaller predators. However, many are still very dangerous, such as the red-bellied piranha. Every piranha has a set of razor-sharp teeth that they use to bite small chunks out of animals. These fish have been known to swim in large **schools** and overwhelm their prey by attacking all at once, stripping the animal to the bone in seconds!

With so many dangerous predators in the water, some fish have developed special defences to protect themselves. The electric eel generates electricity using two special **organs** in its body. It uses these organs to defend itself against attacks by releasing a quick burst of electricity into the water.

Electric eels can deliver a shock of up to 860 volts.

The Amazon Rainforest

The largest rainforest in the world is the Amazon rainforest in South America, which stretches across nine countries and covers 5,500,000 square kilometres of land. Most of the world's **oxygen**, which all animals need to survive, is made in the Amazon rainforest. It makes up between 20% and 30% of the world's supply of oxygen.

The Amazon River is the largest river in the world and is home to at least 3,000 different species of fish. It is also home to the second largest **freshwater** fish in the world, called the Arapaima.

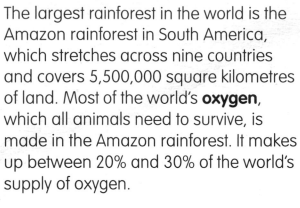

Arapaima

About 10% of all of the species in the world live in the Amazon rainforest. This includes 40,000 different species of plant.

The Amazon is under threat from **deforestation** and it is shrinking fast. Over the past 40 years, 20% of the forest has been cut down.

Cut down trees in the Amazon rainforest in Brazil

Around 400 **tribes** still live in the Amazon rainforest. It is believed that over 50 of these tribes have never come into contact with the modern world.

This fisherman is from the Kamayura tribe.

The Pacific Temperate Rainforests

The Pacific temperate rainforests, which are found on the north-west coast of North America, is the largest of the seven temperate rainforests in the world.

The tallest trees in the world, called redwoods or sequoias, grow in this temperate zone. They can grow to be as much as 91 metres tall. Many of these trees can live to be over 1000 years old!

A Sequoia Tree in Sequoia National Park, California

Pacific Temperate Forest

Nurse Log, Olympic National Park

Nurse logs are an important habitat in the Pacific temperate rainforest. When the large redwood trees fall to the ground, their trunks rot and provide new **seedlings** with a **fertile** place to grow. The Pacific temperate rainforests have lost a lot of their size in the last 70 years. In some areas, over 90 percent of the redwoods have been cut down.

Deforestation in British Columbia, Canada

Saving the Rainforest

Many of the rainforests across the world are under threat. They once covered over 14% of the world's land, but now rainforests make up less than half of that. This is due to deforestation.

IT IS IMPORTANT THAT WE LOOK AFTER THE RAINFORESTS AS IT IS ESTIMATED THAT AROUND 50% OF THE WORLD'S WILDLIFE LIVES IN A RAINFOREST.

Rainforests are not just important to the animals that live in them – they are important for every living thing on the planet. Rainforests supply up to 30% of all the world's oxygen. On top of this, they also absorb and get rid of carbon dioxide, which is one of the gases that is helping to cause **global warming**.

How Can You Help?

One way to help stop trees in rainforests from being cut down is to make sure that you recycle all your paper. At least 30% of all the trees that are cut down are used to make paper. So don't throw your paper in the bin – recycle it instead! When paper is recycled, it means that we can use it again, which means that fewer trees need to be cut down.

Large areas in tropical rainforests are also cut down to make room for farmland. But about one third of the food in world is not eaten and instead goes to waste. If we cut down on the amount of food that we waste, then less trees would have to be cut down to make farmland. Because of this, we should all try to waste as little food as possible.

Quick Quiz and Useful Links

Quick Quiz

How many centimetres of rainfall does the Amazon rainforest receive each year?

What are the four levels of the rainforest?

What adaptation do gibbons have to help them climb?

How can you tell the difference between a Jaguar and a Leopard?

How do pitcher plants catch their food?

What is the largest rainforest in the world?

Useful Links

Check out these awesome websites for more facts about the rainforests:

ngkids.co.uk

bbc.co.uk/nature/habitats

gowild.wwf.org.uk/

rainforest-alliance.org/everyday-actions

Glossary

acid	a liquid that can break down objects into small pieces
adapted	changed over time to suit different conditions
algae	living things that are like plants, but have no roots, stems, leaves or flowers
antibiotic	a substance that stops germs and other small living things from growing
climate	the common weather in a certain place
deforestation	the cutting down and removal of trees in a forest
digest	to break down food into things that can be absorbed and used by the body
environment	natural world
equator	the imaginary line around the Earth that is equal distance from the North and South Poles
fertile	soil that is able to grow strong, healthy crops
freshwater	water that does not have a lot of salt in it, unlike seawater
global warming	the slow rise of the Earth's temperature
larvae	a type of young insect that must grow and change before it can reach its adult form
organs	parts of a living thing that have specific, important functions
oxygen	a natural gas that all living things need in order to survive
poisonous	dangerous or deadly when eaten
predators	animals that hunt other animals for food
prey	animals that are hunted by other animals for food
reproduce	to produce young through the act of mating
schools	large groups of fish or sea mammals
seedlings	young plants
species	a group of very similar animals or plants that are capable of producing young together
spores	tiny seed-like organisms that will grow into new fungi
temperate zones	two areas on Earth's surface that lie between the equator and the Poles, where the weather is cold in the winter and warm in the summer
traits	features or characteristics that help an animal survive
tribes	groups of people linked together by family, society, religion or community
wingspan	the distance the between the tips of a bird's wings

Index